Life's Not Over Until God Says It's Over

Patricia Jones-Taylor

Published By
KWP Publishing Company
An Imprint of Kingdom Word Publications
Albion, Michigan 49224

Printed in the U.S.A

Life's Not Over Until God Says It's Over
Copyright © 2011 Patricia Jones-Taylor
All Rights Reserved

ISBN: 978-0-9712916-7-6
Library of Congress Control Number: 2011921152

Unless otherwise noted, all scripture references are taken from the New American Standard Bible

No portion of this book may be reproduced, stored in a retrieval system, or transmitted in any form or by any means electronic, mechanical photocopy, recording, or any other means except for brief quotations in printed reviews, without the prior written permission of the publisher.

Cover Design WriteRight Publishing Services
Professional Copy Edit Services by KingdomScribe Services
Photography by Elder Fred Jemison Agape Images Photography

Table of Contents

Acknowledgements	v
Apostle M.W Taylor	xi
What Others Are Saying	xiii
Introduction	1
• Being Ready For The Rapture	5
Chapter 1	9
Chapter 2 Growing Up	15
• God Is Real	16
• Other Victories	18
Chapter 3 My Family	21
Chapter 4 Experiencing His Power	25
• Receiving The Power	29
• A New Church and Called Into The Ministry	31
• Searching for More Leads to Meeting My Husband	32
Chapter 5 My Husband, Wayne	37
Chapter 6 Ministry Works	47
Chapter 7 My Heart Attack On Christmas 2009	49
• A Lose-Lose Situation	52

- Calling 'The Specialist'   54

Chapter 8 The Out of Body Experience   57

- The Heart Surgeon   61

Chapter 9 Obedience   65

Chapter 10   77

ACKNOWLEDGEMENTS

Special thanks to my youngest sister Rhonda Renaye Jones Warren, who could be referred to as Grandmother. She has assumed the role of the entire siblings' mother and my mother's mother. We have allowed her to assume the title, because she not only gives the commands but she is on the front line to make it happen.

She is a mover and shaker. During my recovery, her stamina was remarkable. She was one of my main caregivers. God used her greatly to minister to me His love as He walked me through my recovery. Her benevolence was not restricted to my recovery. She is the kind of person when a need presents itself, if it is in her power to meet it – physically or financially – she will make the sacrifice to meet the need, with no explanation needed. Renaye, thank you again for allowing me and others to see the love of Jesus demonstrated (Matthew 25:34-36).

Special thanks to my best friend of over thirty years, Sharon Faye Howze. Proverbs 31:10 asks the question, "Who can find a virtuous woman? For her price is far above rubies". Finding the characteristics that Sharon possesses as a friend is non-comparable. Proverbs 17:17 states a friend love at all times. This is the kind of friend that Sharon has been toward me for over thirty years. She has stuck closer than a brother or a natural sister (Proverbs 18:24).

During my recovery was the first time in twenty years that I did not call her to tell her where I would be carrying her for her birthday. She has never forgotten my birthday, or my husband's, or any of my four children's birthdays, nor my wedding anniversary. I genuinely forgot her birthday when I was recovering. Instead, my friend went out and bought me a gift and a card on her birthday thanking the Lord for sparing my life. Inside the card she wrote, *"this has been the best gift that I have ever received for my birthday; the gift of life of my friend. Thank You, Lord"*. And naturally we cried together. Thank you, Sharon, for defining the word *"friend"*.

Special thanks to my body (husband) Apostle Merlin Wayne Taylor, from which I (rib) was taken. When God gave me a husband, He indeed gave me a man who understands his role as a husband. He truly loves me as God loves His church and gave Himself for it. Before my illness I knew my husband loved me but during my illness I found out just how much. He did not leave my side neither day nor night. I must confess at night I became a little selfish. In other words, misery loves company. I couldn't sleep so I wouldn't let him sleep; and he didn't divorce me. Thank you, Taylor for loving me not because of but in spite of. Thank you for understanding ministry and praying me through to purpose.

Special thanks to my four children; Elijah, Elisha, Victoria and Jesse for helping your Dad carry the load while I was recuperating and for taking care of each other so that your Dad had more time to take care of me. Thank you, Taylor children for being children of the Word.

Special thanks to my mother, Melville Jones and Father, Rallis Jones Sr. (deceased) for being a part of God's plan to birth a daughter that God would use to bring forth a message in 2011 of His Son, Jesus Christ, return to the earth. Thank you, mother for raising nine children to the best of your ability and teaching us about Jesus. I love you, mother and to my mother-in-law, Mattie Taylor (MeMa), for raising a son that would one day grow up to hear and obey the voice of the Lord and to position himself for ministry. Thank you, MeMa, for the love.

All of my seven siblings especially my eldest sister, Bessie McMillan, who in nineteen years has never missed sending a birthday card containing the amount of money for the number of their age to each of my children. Thank you, sister for helping make their birthdays special each year.

Special thanks to Rallis (Bettie) Jones, Lawrence (need wife), Marilyn (Antone) Lane, Allen (Roselyn) Jones, Doris Richardson, Danny L. Jones Sr., deceased (Angela Cotton Jones), Rhonda (Eugene) Warren and my niece, Lanye (James) Webb, who called everyday to see if her Uncle Wayne had something to eat and who encouraged me to tell my story to the world.

To my nephew Dwight Scruggs (D.J), who said I had to mention his name somewhere – anywhere in my book. It's yours for the asking D.J. Thanks to all of my other family members for standing with me and for showing your love in your own way.

Special thanks to my very dear, (late) friend, James Jones who died of a heart attack on September 6, 2010, Labor Day. We were very close friends for years. He and his wife Lorena, had come to visit with me during my recovery. We talked extensively about my out of body experience, not realizing that his rapture was sooner than I expected. I will forever cherish our friendship and the genuine love he showed to my children.

Aunt Susie and Uncle Herman Crumb, I have never known two people so dedicated to true ministry away from the spotlight. God indeed has your reward.

Special thanks to my very dear cousin, Anthony Eaton, for all of the encouragement. You truly inspired me to obey God by getting this message out; that Jesus is soon to return. Thanks for all your support.

Special thanks to H.E.R.S Women Ministry. Thank you ladies for helping to hold up my arms to fulfill purpose in **Honoring Every Resurrected Sister.**

To HIS WORD Ministries Church Family, you all truly showed your love to us during my recovery. God had to have handpicked you all for us. Thank you all for the prayers, visits, gifts, food, comforting words and most of all for being on post.

Elders Frank and Bonita Brown, Bonnie and children, for carrying on the ministry, as well as, Roebuck Auto Service and Tire Business in our absence – as though we were there; thank you for the love and support.

Special thanks to our Godson and musician, Renaurd Gulley, Jr. for staying the course. To Joe Evans, Tony Pugh, Jr. and the Pugh Family (Deacon Jerry, Mother Deanna, Desiree and Austin for your commitment to ministry), you are indeed steadfast.

Sister Krishun Brown and family for all you did and gave to help with our transition.

To Prophetess Candace Collier, who set her face toward the wall until she heard a word from heaven; that, "This sickness was not unto death", a confirming word.

Jones Family Monday Prayer Group and my only living aunt, Katie Oates, Mobile, AL, Evangelist Cynthia Hall (Intercessor) and son Chris Hall, thank you, Cynthia for uprooting from your home to come and help take care of my children during my recovery. Cynthia, you are a friend indeed.

Our spiritual children, Bishop Daniel and Pastor Terryle Parker; we are proud to call you our spiritual children. Pastor Terryle you have always been just a phone call away. Thanks for all you continue to do for us. Pastors Alfred and Viola Broadnax, Viola, thanks for helping to edit and proofread my Book. You all are indeed our God-given children.

To Evangelist Damon and Jennifer Davis Graham, thanks for unconditional love and thanks, Jennifer for standing the test of time with us.

Prophet Leon Lee, a radical pastor of power, and his wife Pastor Linda Lee (founder of S.W.A.T. Ministries) who held on to God in prayer until He brought His 'preach brother!' wife back, thank you Lee(s).

Thanks to Adrienne and Theo Nicholas, loving grandparents to Jeremiah spent the second half of Jeremiah's birthday at the hospital interceding with Apostle Taylor for my recovery.

Thank you, Sister Terri Harris and Meagan who stepped up to the plate in intercession and providing daily meals to my family and especially for giving Victoria a great fifteenth birthday celebration when I didn't know I was still in the world.

Pastor Edward Kirkland (Atlanta, GA), friend and co-laborer of the Gospel for over twenty years – who called weekly after hearing of my illness. He pressed the issue of obeying God in a timely manner. "Let's get this story out". He also introduced me to my now publisher, Pastor Tim Kurtz. Thanks Pastor Kirkland.

To Al & Denise Perdue, close and compassionate friends for over thirty-five years (Pervending Drinks and Snacks Company).

Special thanks to the staff of Shelby Baptist Hospital (Second Floor), Doctors, Nurses and Support. Beware of entertaining strangers; you might just be entertaining or caring for an Angel unaware (Hebrews 13:2). Thanks for all the compassion. I told you all that I would not forget your labor of love.

                                          Pastor Patricia J. Taylor
                                          January 2011

As I began to think back upon the events of the past Christmas season (2009), I can hear the words of a well-known song (How Great is our God, Sing with me, How Great, How Great is our God). Truly, this is the testament my wife and I have shared over the course of our lives together. We have seen our God show Himself strong in our behalf on so many occasions. They are too numerous to tell in this setting alone, and this one is no different.

We did not anticipate or expect Christmas 2009 to occur as it did. It came without any warning naturally or prophetically. We were thrust into another opportunity to trust God like never before. My wife had never been seriously ill or hospitalized before (except during the delivery of our four children), and she was not taking any medication. So upon hearing the different Doctors say words like heart attack, coronary disease, etc. it was hard to accept this as truth concerning her.

So much happened over the course of those nine days that she was hospitalized. So much more happened after arriving home that from my vantage point it would be another book in order to tell all that God did. As you read her account of how God awesomely moved and spoke to her; allow His Word to penetrate your heart and make the decision to get right with Him before it's too late. This event has changed the course of lives and ministry once again, to impact and to advance the Kingdom of God like never before. I will forever be thankful to God for hearing my cry in that season, a simple cry, "Please Lord, not now", and as in times past He was faithful to hear and answer with signs, wonders, and miracles following.

> **Apostle M.W. Taylor**
> **His Word Ministries International**

WHAT OTHERS ARE SAYING...

Pastor Patricia Taylor is a woman of God and a mighty prayer warrior. She exhibits a zeal and love for God's people that is evidenced by her constant overflow of preaching, teaching, exhorting, and comforting God's people. Her relationship and fellowship with God is reflected by her love and compassion for others. We are living in a very serious time and we must "cry loud and spare not."

Pastor Taylor's divine encounter substantiates the fact that time is "drawing nigh." We should admonish that – he that hath an ear, let him hear what the Spirit saith unto the churches as in Revelation 3:6. When I prophesied that she would write a book, it was totally under the supernatural unction of the Holy Spirit. All Glory goes to God. We must endeavor to keep the unity of the faith. I am confident of this very thing that God will continue to perform the good work He has begun in Pastor Taylor's life until the return of Jesus Christ. I am also fully persuaded that nothing can separate us from the love of Jesus Christ our Lord. I am humbled to be a part of God's plan in this hour.

> Chief Apostle Israel Jones Sr., DD/PhD
> Chief Apostle and Senior Pastor
> Tabernacle of the Word Church
> Birmingham, Alabama
> Author of several books, including:
> *Change Your Clothes, We Have Never Been This Way Before, Pride Comes Before the Fall, Understanding Covering, Are You Mature Enough To Marry, Warfare Prayers,* and *Understanding the Five-Fold Ministry*

While the interest of the body of Christ may lie in other areas of scripture, it seems that the Lord is trying to get the church to place serious studies surrounding the pearly gates of heaven. This book is written with a subject matter that has disappeared from present-day pulpits. The horrendous trial Pastor Taylor went through should have caused her death, but for thousands, this literary work may produce a spiritual awakening.

To think of the horrifying number of those who entered the Heavenly courts of God's inspection, as Pastor Taylor did and the records there indicated that there was no attempt of an effectual personal relationship with the Lord, may have been horrendous. The unbelievable reality of facing eternal damnation, based on words written in the chronicles of Heaven is a wakeup call to many. I give God the Glory for bringing Pastor Taylor through such a terrifying trial, but it seems as though God had a higher purpose.

I truly believed that the purpose of her sickness was to bring her into a place where God would show her some marvelous things in Heaven. Moreover, the things that Pastor Taylor saw in heaven are a message for today's easygoing church. Churches where grace may be over emphasized, and relationship is a thing of the past.

The Bible says in Hebrews 10:26, *"Dear friends, if we deliberately continue sinning after we have received knowledge of the truth, there is no longer any sacrifice that will cover these sins "*(New Living Translation).

Although, the Lord has published two books through my life experiences, Christianity vs. Paganism and Doors Of The Mind, what God is doing with Pastor Taylor is of the most urgent need for today's church. We are fortunate to have a person who stood in the presence of the holy gates of God, who has been sent back to warn the body of Christ about those books. Congratulations Pastor Taylor and I pray for the success of this work.

Bishop Demetrics Roscoe

The book of Revelation opens with: *"This is a revelation from Jesus Christ, which God gave him to show his servants the events that must soon take place"* (Revelation 1:1 NLT).

Pastor Patricia Taylor has intimate and personal insight from the judgment room of heaven for the church today, even as each of the Seven Churches in Revelation received a clear and specific word through John the Revelator from Christ for his day. Both Pastor Taylor and Apostle John surprise how timely and imperative it is to make the necessary spiritual adjustments to prepare for the coming of Christ for their generation.

As for Pastor Patricia, her life and walk with Christ only validates what she experienced on the operating table, and what she has placed in this book. Anyone in search of the truth, Pastor Patricia is not one to flatter, fabricate, or fascinate you into the promises of God. Read her life experience and become a believer in the only true, holy, and risen Savior and Lord, Jesus Christ.

> Lisa Langie
> Pastor, Faith Life, Inc
> Founder of Overcoming Faith Outreach Center
> Founder of Rachel's Kids

While reading Chapter 8 of *Life's Not Over*, I found the life a person living in the earth as evidence of one day we will all stand before the Judge that is to say where will you spend eternity.

I found this book to be a compelling source of information as well as an account of infallible doctrine based on Biblical happenings. In Chapter 8 particularly of *Life's Not Over*, I read about the outer body experience while in surgery, what happened when the spirit of the life came outside of Pastor Patricia's body and she looked down on herself lying on the table. Suddenly she was carried into a courtroom where she described the Judge who is ultimately God. The Prosecuting Attorney whom had already served the guilty verdict against a child of God implying she could not keep the law because of the things done in flesh. The Bible declares we are not under the law, but by Grace we are saved.

Also in the courtroom were one witness and her defense Attorney (Advocate) who ruled in her favor. God overrules the Prosecuting Attorney. Even though God knows we can't be perfect in the flesh, that's why we have an Advocate our lawyer in a courtroom and by His blood we have been redeemed from the law of sin and death.

After the ruling she was not found guilty but at last free to receive a crown of righteousness. She had a choice to make – whether to go to heaven or to return to earth. Her decision was, "I will wait and be raptured up with Christ", relating to 1Thessalonians 4:17-18. Yes, the Judge opens this big book that records the day of rapturing the Church is soon. Her commission was to come back to earth and preach the Gospel; the Kingdom of God is at hand (Matthew 10:7).

As we live in this world, we as Christians know the end time is near. The second coming of Christ (The Advent) the end of the world is nearing. I know Pastor Patricia Taylor, a devout Christian, who loves God and is always encouraging the people of God. This book is inspired of the Holy Ghost, and reading Chapter 8 has inspired me to rise upward in God. I believe everyone that reads this book will definitely have their lives impacted. I have reserved in the archives in my personal library room for this book.

Christ Messenger
Pastor Terrlye Parker
Feed My Sheep Ministries

Truly, God is the Perfect Matchmaker by uniquely joining Apostle Taylor and Pastor Patricia in holy matrimony; one coming into the union as an only child, and the other the seventh child of nine. As a holy couple that would be anointed to fight the spiritual forces of darkness as good soldiers of

Jesus Christ, this team was prepared for the sudden attack on Pastor Patricia's life.

Sent by the enemy to "kill, steal, and destroy," the attack had to return to its owner, the devil, with very sad news: "I could not accomplish what I was sent to do." As an imitator of God, the enemy can send a word, but only the Word of God is effectual ALL THE TIME when it is sent on an assignment.

Pastor Patricia's book lucidly reveals the power of God's Word on assignment, and is replete with instances portraying God's amazing power to turn adversities into triumphs – from a wayward son to the climactic "heart attack" – all ending in praise and victory. This woman of God has something to shout about! After you read this book, I am sure that you, too, will be shouting and giving God the praise, as His word, not man's, is final, authoritative, and efficacious!

> Pastor Anthony F. Eaton
> Senior Pastor, Kingdom Mission Church
> Raleigh, NC
> Author of *Money My Servant for Kingdom Expansion* and *Understanding and Overcoming Lusts*

As a young child, I can still remember standing in church singing the simple chorus: *"Trust and obey, for there's no other way to be happy in Jesus, but to trust and obey."* As I have had the privilege to get to know Patricia Taylor, it's become clear that she is a woman characterized by the words of that hymn so profoundly penned centuries ago. Wife, mother, Sunday school teacher, and yes... even heart attack survivor, Mrs. Taylor has experienced the secret to true contentment and she passionately shares it through her life and now through the writing of this book—a book born out of faith and out of response to her Savior's call.

As the reader will quickly discover as he walks with Mrs. Taylor through the pages of her life, happiness in Jesus does not always mean ease or comfort. Nor does it necessarily mean perfect health or lack of relational struggle. What it *does* mean is that for the one who knows Jesus Christ, life on this earth has meaning and purpose. Intimacy with Him is not only our highest call; it is our highest delight and it is the reason why people like Mrs. Taylor share their story with us.

In John's Revelation he writes, *"Behold, He is coming with the clouds, and every eye will see Him, and even those who pierced Him; and all the tribes of the earth will mourn over Him. Even so. Amen"* (1:7, NASB). As sons and daughters of Adam, each of us stands condemned for we all have pierced the beloved Son of God. Yet, this same Jesus, through His perfect earthly life, His substitutionary death, and His victory over Hell and the grave has provided a way by which we might be saved. The One from whom we alienated ourselves and declared our enemy has reconciled us to Himself so that we might now be called friends and may worship Him around His throne both now and one day with Him face to face.

May your heart be encouraged as you learn more of this Good News through the life of His faithful servant, Mrs. Taylor.

M. Heath Hale, MD, MPH, CAQSM
Shelby Sports and Family Medicine

Patricia Jones Taylor has done a great job with this book. It will speak to your heart in a big way because the Holy Spirit is on the pages of this book. It shows how God can use a willing vessel for His good – a chosen vessel from her mother's womb, to share the Good News. She has always had a passion for souls and wants to see people come to Christ.

I have personally known her for three decades, and her passion has not changed for God. No wonder God has chosen to visit her in such a unique way through her spiritual experience. The Bible says in Acts 2:17-18, *"In the last days, says God, I will pour out My Spirit, on all flesh, your sons and daughters shall prophesy"* (speak things out of the heart of God). I also believe that Jesus is coming soon and we must be ready for His return.

So I know you will enjoy this powerful book.

Pastor Edward Kirkland
Faith To Faith Church
Atlanta, Georgia

I have known Pastor Patricia J. Taylor for over 20 years. She has a strong prophetic gift that operates mightily in her life. I was there at the hospital when the doctor told the family about her heart condition. I prayed with the family for a miracle healing in her body. I went back into the monitor room. I prayed with her that she shall live and not die and declared the works of the Lord according to Psalm 118:17. She told me that it is well. "I have made peace with God."

I believe God allowed her to experience that out of body experience like Paul according to 2Corinthians 12:4. That she could tell his people that Jesus is soon to come. The Holy Bible says that this Gospel shall be preached to all nations as a witness, then shall the end be, according to Matthew 24:14.

        Pastor Leon Lee, Jr.
        Church of Judah International
        Tuscaloosa, Alabama

Introduction

In 2004, it was prophesied to me that I would write a book and many would be blessed by it. Two different prophets in two different locations spoke the same word over me. The first time, it did not impact me much. The second time when the exact words were spoken, I had to stop and take notice. I realize that there are some today who are skeptics when it comes to the gift of prophesy - due to misrepresentation of the gift or lack of information, but the Bible tells us in 1Thessalonians 5:20, "...to not to despise prophesying."

The first thing that came to my mind was, "How can this thing be?" This is the same question Mary, the mother of Jesus, inquired from the angel when she was told that she would conceive. She knew that something would take place that had to be beyond her doing (Luke 1:34). Likewise, I knew writing a book would be beyond me.

My second thought was what or how would I go about writing a book? What would I write about? At that time there was nothing out of the ordinary in my life. I am a wife, mother, daughter, and sister in an all-American Christian family, going about serving Jesus while experiencing the everyday trials of maintaining the believer's victory.

But in 2010, I was given a story to tell. God spoke to me, as He did John, in the first chapter of the book of Revelation, "...the things that you have seen and heard, write them in a book..." (Revelation 1:11). So here we are...

As I entered into prayer and sought the heart of God concerning the intent of this book, which is to awake the mind of the people to realize that God is soon to return, and that they must be ready. I also presented to the Lord, what about those who will not believe, or have said in their heart, "I have heard that before that Jesus is soon to return?" Some have said, I have heard Jesus is on His way back since I was a child, and now I am grown."

How do we respond to these comments? My immediate response has been that Noah preached one hundred and twenty years announcing *"to get ready, it is going to rain"* (Genesis 6:3-7). People did not believe then, and did not make ready. Many died because of unbelief.

The Lord gave me 2Peter 3:1-12:

This is now, "beloved, the second letter I am writing to you in which I am stirring up your sincere mind by way of reminder. that you should remember the words spoken beforehand by the holy prophets and the commandment of the Lord and Savior spoken by your Apostles. Know this first of all, that in the last days mockers will come with their mocking, following after their own lusts and saying, <u>*"Where is the promise of His coming? For ever since the fathers fell asleep, all continues just as it was from the beginning of creation.*</u> *For when they maintain this it escapes their notice that by the word of God the heavens existed long ago and the earth was formed out of water and by water through which the world at that time was destroyed being flooded with water. But the present heavens and earth by His word are being reserved for fire, kept for the day of judgment and destruction of ungodly men, 8 But do not let this one fact escape your notice, beloved, that with the Lord, one day is as a thousand years, and a thousand years as one day. But know this, The Lord is not slow about His promise, as some count slowness, but is patient toward you, not wishing for any to perish but for all to come to repentance.*

But the day of the Lord will come like a thief in which the heavens will pass away with a roar and the elements will be destroyed with intense heat. And the earth and its works will be burned up. Since all these things are to be destroyed in this way, what sort of people ought you to be in holy conduct and godliness. looking for and hastening the coming of the day of God, on account of which the heavens will be destroyed by burning and the elements will melt with intense heat! (Make Ready!)

But according to His promise, we are looking for new heavens and a new earth, in which righteousness dwells. Therefore, beloved, since you look for these things, be diligent to be found by Him in peace, spotless and blameless.

"...and blessed is she who believed that there would be a fulfillment of what had been spoken to her by the lord (Luke 1:45).

God can't lie. He's coming back!

Therefore since we have so great a cloud of witnesses surrounding us, let us also lay aside every encumbrance, and the sin which so easily entangles us, and let us run with endurance, the race that is set before us. Fixing our eyes on

Jesus, the author and perfecter of faith, who for the joy set before Him endured the cross, despising the shame, and has sat down at the right hand, of the throne of God. For consider Him who has endured such hostility by sinners against Himself, so that you may not grow weary and lose heart (Hebrews 12:1-3).

Therefore, since we receive a kingdom which cannot be shaken, let us show gratitude, by which we may offer to God an acceptable service (a holy life) with reverence (commitment) and awe (worship). For our God is a consuming fire. (Hebrews 12: 28-29)

Being Ready For The Rapture

One of the hardest things to let go of is a love one who you are now separated from. You miss that individual dearly. Michael Jackson wrote a song that summed it up in a heartfelt way "Gone too soon".

As I stated before, I have lost many dear relatives, but none like my youngest brother, Danny and my Dad. But my strength and consolation in our separation have been according to God's Word, I will see them again.

Every time I read the newspaper and I look at the obituary page, I see individuals who have been raptured away. It is a reminder that God's word is true, where Jesus states, "if I go away" (leave the earth) and He did, "I will come again to receive you unto myself" (those who die in the Lord). We see every day that individuals are raptured away, but there will soon be a universal rapture that none will escape.

As a Pastor, many times I have had to comfort others through the loss of a love one. I have come to accept that nothing reaches the heart to mend this brokenness like prayer and time.

When I seem loss for words, I have to be reminded that God is the God of all comfort, and that His Word, not our opinions, or sharing our encounters of losing our love ones will lessen their pain. God releases comfort through His rhema or logos word.

He states in 1Thessalonians 4:13-18,

> But we do not want you to be uninformed, brethren, about those who are asleep, that you may not grieve, as do the rest who have no hope. V14 For if we believe that Jesus died and rose again even so God will bring with Him those who have fallen asleep in Jesus. For this we say to you by the word of the Lord, that we, who are alive and remain until the coming of the Lord, shall not precede those who have fallen asleep. For the Lord, Himself, will descend from heaven with a shout, with the voice of the archangel, and with the trumpet of God; and the dead in Christ shall rise first. Then, we who are alive and remain shall be caught up together with them (your deceased love ones) in the clouds

to meet the Lord in the air, and thus we shall always be with the Lord. Therefore comfort one another with these words...

It's Not Over until God Says It's Over.....

CHAPTER 1

Many times the credibility of a story is based on whose it is and whether or not you can relate to the person.

I am fifty-three years old and the wife of twenty-one years, to a wonderful, God-fearing man, Wayne. I am a retired educator from the Birmingham Board of Education after 28 years of service. I began as a secretary with them right after receiving my Associate Degree in Business from Southern Junior College. I enjoyed my job but it did not allow me to make the money I desired. Therefore, while yet working, I earned both my Bachelor and Master Degrees. God truly favored me during this time.

He allowed me to attend Graduate School in Huntsville, Alabama while yet working in Birmingham. I met three other determined students from Birmingham who also desired a higher education and together we carpooled, back and forth, three nights per week for two years. We were truly strength and encouragement to one another. The task was not easy but we were relentless to get our degrees and it paid-off. I became the Director of the community school which was very productive for me – both in experience and finances.

I was born and raised in Birmingham, Alabama. I was educated in the Birmingham School System. I am the seventh of nine children. I have four sisters (none like them anywhere). They believe in family-ties. We have had our differences through the years, mainly because of my spiritual convictions, which they did not fully understand; yet, they love me as their sister. We have a scheduled sisters' trip, to various states, every two years. We all look forward to this time to get away.

I have three living brothers; very astute and witty. My youngest brother has gone on to be with the Lord. The eldest two brothers and the youngest one were a lot alike: loving and caring in their own way. However, the third born, Allen, had to have been cut from a different cloth when it comes to relating to others and being task oriented.

My brother was saved and spirit-filled six years after I was filled. My request to the Lord was, "Father if You would just save and fill at least one of my siblings, I'll go all the way for you" and God did just that.

He used me to go to Biloxi, Mississippi where Allen and his wife, Roselyn, were living. Roselyn and I had attended high school together. She had come to Birmingham prior to my visit to Biloxi. God used me first to share the good news of the gospel with her, upstairs in my parents' home. She received Christ in my bedroom and was filled with His Spirit there. Less than a year later, God sent me to Biloxi to visit and Allen received salvation and the Holy Spirit.

Allen was a devout Baptist. He did not believe that 'speaking in tongues' was for today's believers and that it did not take such a consecrated life to live for Jesus. His words were, "It does not take all of that". But that day Allen was reacquainted with the Father and the Son and personally introduced to the Holy Spirit. He came to realize that the Holy Spirit is the third person of the Trinity. He realized that the Holy Spirit is the personality of the Father. After his conversion, he could only say, "It's real."

Danny, my youngest brother, died at the age of forty-five. He and I were very close growing up. He was very protective of me; although, I was two years older than he. God had delivered him from alcoholism. He had been clean for about four years prior to his death. During his recovery he had moved back home with my parents.

One thing I asked the Lord, in accordance to His Word, was that He would save my family members. He stated that if I believe on Him that I will be saved and my loved ones (Acts16:31). Danny, through the faithfulness of Jesus Christ, had gotten his life together. He accepted Jesus as his Savior and Lord and had become the store manager for the Salvation Army.

One Saturday after work he arrived home and told my mother that he was very tired. He continued with his usual activities that day. After retiring for the night, God called him home sometime during the night. He died in his sleep.

It was Sunday morning *(what an awesome day to check out)*. My mother said that she did not attempt to wake him for church since he seemed to have been so tired the night before. After she and the rest of the family returned home, she called him to come and eat dinner. When he did not respond she went to see why. She found that he had checked out of this earthly house and checked into his eternal resting home.

Although, we did not have an autopsy done; my Doctor, after my heart attack, strongly believed that a heart attack could have been the cause of Danny's death.

Praise the Lord! God is faithful. I was so blessed to see God keep His Word by saving Danny before his departure. I believe that the Lord took Danny home with Him in order to maintain his right standing with Him. Now he is in eternity with the Lord.

My father died in 1999 at the age of 74. He died in his sleep, too. There was no autopsy done, but a strong possibility of a heart attack, also. He died a day before Thanksgiving.

In his earlier years he started attending church but by his fruit and lifestyle, one could tell that he did not have a relationship with Jesus Christ. As many others today; he had a form of godliness but denied the power, II Timothy 3:5 the ability to allow the Word to bring about a change in his life.

But thanks unto God, four years prior to his passing, God allowed me to pray with my father and lead him in the sinner's prayer. This was during the same time that we stood in agreement concerning Danny's deliverance and renounced the generational curse of alcoholism.

My father and my mother were faithful ushers in the family church. Dad was the chairman of the Usher Board for over five years. He took his position very seriously. Upon his departure, the Usher Board was named after him, Rallis Jones Sr. Usher Ministry. Once again, God showed his faithfulness.

Last, but certainly not least, I have a very vibrant 84-year-old mother; who will probably not appreciate my telling her age. She truly does not look or carry herself reflecting her age. As she loves to say, "She is a very blessed woman". My father died at the age of 74. They had been married fifty-five years. It was very hard for my mother to go on with life after my father's departure, but she knew she had not finished her course, so she had to fight on.

There was a time when she did not want to go on without him. But as she stated, she knew her children needed her, and we do. We have learned a lot from our mother through her examples of diligence, honor, strength and wisdom demonstrated in her everyday life (Proverbs 31:26, 27).

CHAPTER 2

Growing up

I was raised to go to church. My parents sent us on the church bus even before they started attending. We were sent to Sunday school, 11 a.m. church service, and then to BTU (Baptist Training Union) which was held on Sunday evenings. The Jones' family children were known for perfect attendance on Sunday. There were nine of us, and my parents seized the opportunity to get a break. In their mind, church was a good, safe and free place, which included transportation to and from, so we were sent out to church every Sunday. However, thanks unto God; they soon joined us with weekly attendance.

My siblings and I were raised in the church. While being faithful to the regulations of the church, God began to deal with me from His Word. I began to read the Bible for myself. My eyes were opening. I began to question the inconsistency in the lives of the members of the church. Why did the Bible say one thing but yet the people did their own thing – and, in my mind it was not addressed.

By the time I was eighteen, I was fed up with the hypocrisy I saw. One day, I sat on my bed, alone in my room, and said out loud, "God, if You are real, show me!" I recall a close minister friend saying, "Be careful for what you ask the Lord for and make sure it is what you want. You might just get it". God did just that. He proceeded to show me that He is real!

God is Real

One day while driving home, I was going down a hill approaching a stop sign. I saw a car ahead of me with two small children standing up on the backseat of the car looking toward the coming traffic. This was before the seat belt law was in effect.

As I was approaching, I gently put my foot on the brake because I was increasing speed. To my amazement, even after attempting to apply pressure to the brakes, the brake pedal went straight to the floor. God took my mind into slow motion. The car was increasing in speed but God allowed me to think, "If I hit the car front of me, it will be pushed into oncoming traffic and these small children could be fatally injured." By this time I was about ten feet away from this car.

I closed my eyes and said, "Jesus!" Suddenly my hands were overshadowed; I turned the steering wheel and there appeared a pathway onto the sidewalk. The car turned into the pathway, the car came about five feet from a big oak tree and stopped. Keep in mind that the brakes were gone. I sat there in amazement. Before I could move, a voice spoke audibly saying, "I Am the God you desire to know. I can stop a car without brakes".

I sat there seemingly paralyzed. I was about one block from home. When I was able to move I ran to my house to tell my family what had happened.

There are so many testimonies I could give when God was introducing Himself to me. Here are a few more!

When I was nineteen years of age, I woke up one morning experiencing serious abdominal pain. I could not straighten my back. I went to the doctor who had me admitted into the hospital. The doctor could not explain what was going on, so he decided to do an exploratory surgery. That night, I rolled out of the hospital bed and kneeled to pray. I told God, "If You are really real, heal my body without the surgery." The next morning I was totally healed. It amazed everyone. I was given some medication and sent home. God is the healer.

Other Victories

In 1979 I was in graduate school; I had just arrived home, parked my car and after I opened my car door I saw a man standing next to me. He asked me for a ride home. He began to plead with me concerning a ride. There was a check in my spirit concerning the man's intention but I still agreed to carry him home. When he got in the car I immediately asked him had he made Jesus Christ both as Savior and Lord of his life. I further began to share my testimony with him about how Christ had come into my life. As we talked, apparently he began to strategize.

To give the short version, we drove around in a circle. There was a second man standing waiting on him. He instructed me to stop the car and pick his friend up. That's when I truly felt something was up. So, I told him that he needed to get out with his friend because I was going home. He pulled out a handgun. He told his friend to get into the car and that I would take them where they needed to go, or I would die there.

Now, here faith shows up again. Imagine a man pointing a gun at you and making a demand. Again he said "Drive the car off now or you will die here". God-faith overshadowed me, and the Spirit of the Living God spoke forth out of me. I said, "When you got into my car I told you that my life was hid in Christ Jesus and I was not my own". I continued to pronounce, "My life is not my own; therefore, you don't have the power to take my life." Then I lifted up my hands toward heaven and began to pray.

Suddenly the guy in the back shouted, "Let me out of here!" The guy in the front asked him, "What is wrong with you"? He replied, "Someone else is in this car with us!" He pushed forth the front seat, jumped out and they both took off running. I can imagine my ministering angels, Goodness and Mercy, stood up tall in the midst of the car. I saw no one, but bless God, they did! (Psalms 23; 32:10).

In 1979 I was driving my family to Mobile for our family reunion. It began to rain very intensely. The tires hit a water puddle and went into a skid. I could not control the steering. As we continued to spin, I looked into the rearview mirror and there was an eighteen-wheeler truck coming over the hill at high speed. He tried to stop but did not see us in time. He crashed into our car at a high rate of speed. Can you believe that God used the truck only to get us out of the spin? No one was hurt not even the car was damaged.

Only a covenant-keeping God, like ours, can do this. Just as He used the whale to house Jonah, He used the eighteen-wheeler to take us out of the spin. God used the whale to bring about His will to hold Jonah unharmed until he surrendered (Jonah 1:17). God used the truck to bring about His divine providence again, that we should not be harmed. Only God can use whosoever or whatsoever to show that He has all power.

All of these miraculous accounts were building faith in me for the day when I would hear the prognosis the doctor would give me regarding my heart attack.

CHAPTER 3

My Family

I have four children – all teenagers.

Elijah, my oldest, is nineteen. I often describe him as my good child. He is very well mannered at all times. He has enlisted in the United States National Guard in January 2011. Elisha, seventeen, is very talented and outgoing. He likes to entertain. Upon graduation from college, he plans to pursue a career in acting. Elisha is the type of person who will succeed at whatever he puts his mind to.

Victoria, my only daughter, is sixteen, petite and beautiful. She enjoys helping others, modeling and basketball. She tries to help me keep the males in check. She does well with all of them with the exception of Jesse, the youngest, who loves to aggravate her. He is fourteen. The last two years have been very challenging for me with Jesse.

He is smart and innovative, but only in what he enjoys. If it does not spark his interest he shuts down and does nothing. He is very good with technology and is very useful around the house when asked, but with everyday school assignments he fails to follow through because he refuses to apply himself. He has indeed caused us to increase our prayer life these last two years.

We later discovered that much of Jesse's impulsive behavior could be contributed to his environment in middle school. He made a drastic improvement transitioning to High School.

Our four children have definitely increased our prayer life. But through them God had proven that He is able to keep that which we commit (dedicate) unto Him until that day, which has been our strength. For we indeed dedicated our children back to Him after their birth.

I am also the grandmother of three-year-old, Jeremiah. He is two-hands full and has already developed a love for music – playing the drums and guitar.

I realize that when satan can't get to us, ministers of the gospel, he in turn goes for that which is dearest to us and more vulnerable, which most of the time is our children. It's like the devil was saying "In your face!" At that moment; I could imagine how Jesus felt on the cross when the chief priest yelled out, "You saved others, now save yourself" (Mark 5:17).

Our children are presently our church musicians, and on their way to total submission to the will of our Father. (Faith is the substance of things hoped for and the evidence of things not seen. Hebrew 11:1)

My ministry to young people has always been effective. In 1986, I became an anti-abortion counselor for a clinic in Birmingham, named 'Save a Life'. There I ministered to hundreds of young people concerning choices and the love of Jesus. Being an educator I was always surrounded by young people. Consequently, I had many opportunities to share the good news of the gospel. I am a firm believer that what I help make happen for someone else; God will make happen for me. This is proven out through scripture, whatsoever a man or woman soweth (put into motion) that shall he or she reap. Galatians 6:7 & 8. So if I direct or redirect someone else love ones, God will send laborers across my family members pathway to show them the right way. God can't lie. Heb. 6:18 His Word is forever settle in heaven. Psalms 119:89

CHAPTER 4

Experiencing His Power

Earlier in my life, through religious acts, I had confessed that I was "born again", only to realize later that I had no fruit. Yes, I went to church faithfully and served in the church, but I did not acknowledge God in my daily walk. I rarely read the Bible outside of church. My standard was the church members rather than the Word of God. God put the plan in motion to draw me to Him.

A close friend of mine called and invited me to attend a new church she was currently attending. She informed me that it was a sanctified, Pentecostal church. She went on to say that she had never experienced the presence of God in the way she had experienced Him there and that no other church experience had changed her life like this one had. She said that she had been born again. I was reluctant at first about going with her, since I was a Baptist and as some have stated, I too was Baptist Born, Baptist Fed and when I die, I too would be Baptist Dead. I came to know that was not scripture and since I wanted to be Spirit Born, Spirit fed and when I Arise Spirit Led. Eventually, I went with her, and my Lord was she right!

At this church, the people were sincere about serving God. They laid down their lives, lifestyles, conversations, way of dressing, and places they frequented for enjoyment for what they believed pleased the Lord. In hindsight, I can now see through their interpretation of the scripture. Although these saints were sincere with what they believed was pleasing to God; they were attempting to reach God through their works. They focused more on the outer-man (the pants, makeup, jewelry and social events). The Bible tells us in Matthew 23:25-26, that it is not the outside of the cup that defiles us, or makes us unclean, rather it is what is inside of us. I chose to joined this church and abide by their rules.

They believed that one must tarry for the Holy Ghost. Yes, Acts second chapter states that they tarried for the Holy Ghost but they failed to realize that the word 'tarry' simply means to wait for the promise. Individuals would go up to the front of the church and sit in certain chairs and were told to keep calling on the name of Jesus. You had to say, "Jesus, Jesus, Jesus, Jesus..." Pause with the music then start up again, "Jesus, Jesus, Jesus, Jesus..."

There could be several people sitting in these chairs at one-time and several 'mothers' in their white clothing standing near you in order to help you while you called on the name of Jesus. The mothers were looking for manifestations such as falling out of the chair and foaming at the mouth. We were taught that this was purging by the Lord. I went on three separate occasions and sat in 'the' chair and called on the name of Jesus.

After my unsuccessful second time of tarrying with no manifestations, one of the dear, sweet, sincere but apparently unlearned mothers said, "Baby, you must still have sin in your life. Do you still wear pants? What about makeup and jewelry?" When I answered, "Yes"; she said, "That's it. That is why you can't get the Holy Spirit because you are still unclean."

Even during that time, being a baby in the Lord that didn't make sense to me; but since I was so hungry for the things of God, I was willing to do whatever it took. Just image this – I went home to my struggling, financially challenged family. I had very little clothing. I bagged up all six pair of my pants. Most of them were given to me through hand-me-downs, but I wore them proudly. I proceeded to get rid of my little jewelry that I cherished, and my few vinyl records which were – as they stated – worldly music. I took all of these items outside and burned them. The mothers had told me I should burn them because I wouldn't want to pass sin on. If it was wrong for me, it would be wrong for others. This type of behavior is what contributed to my parents thinking that I was in some kind of cult or was brainwashed.

I returned to the church on the next meeting night. I went to the altar when it was time to tarry and call on the name of the Lord. I strutted up there proudly knowing that I would fall out of the chair and get the Holy Ghost. After all, I had earned it. I had burned my worldly goods, but much to my disappointment, as I called on Jesus with every fiber of my being for a very lengthy amount of time, nothing happened.

I was very angry and frustrated. The first thing I wanted to do was to slap all those mothers standing around the altar for false information; and to give two slaps to the mother who told me personally to burn my pants and other things, all for naught (smile, just kidding, thank God for deliverance over our thought life).

I left the church in tears. I did not want to hear anything from any of those people. After I arrived home, I went straight to my bedroom. I knew I could not talk to my parents about this because they were already convinced that I was in some kind of cult. So I went to my bedroom and went to sleep. But the next night! All day long there was a peaceful spirit over me. I couldn't explain it, but that night I felt led to stay in my room. I felt something good was going to happen to me.

I tried to fix my chairs like they had them at the church. I sat in one of the chairs and began to call on the name of Jesus like they did at the church. I put a cover on the side of the chair in case I fell out (smile). I began clapping my hands to the tempo of calling on Jesus. I did this for about thirty minutes. Again nothing happened. Again, I was hurt, but this time I said out loud, "Jesus, save me; I want to know You". Suddenly things started happening.

There was a holy hush that came over my bedroom. I fell to my knees and began to weep. When I stood up there was an uncontrollable dance that got into my feet, and an unspeakable joy filled my heart. I knew I had experienced a visitation from the Holy Spirit. I looked at my hands and they looked new then I looked at my feet and they did too. My heart had been changed. There was such a great hunger to know God. I had become a new creation in Christ Jesus (2Corinthians 5:17).

Receiving Power

A month later I went to visit a different church in downtown Birmingham. There was a young man sitting in the service (now Pastor Kirkland). After the service he came over to me and asked had I received the Baptism of the Holy Ghost with the evidence of speaking in other tongues. I told him that I had not spoken in tongues but I knew I had been born again, in my room, about four weeks ago. The young man proceeded to tell me how Jesus wanted to fill me with the Holy Spirit. He asked for my phone number. He called me the next day and began to go over some scriptures with me related to receiving the Holy Spirit.

These scriptures taught me who the Holy Ghost is (John 14:26), the benefits of having the Holy Ghost in my life (Roman 8:26), and how to receive Him (Luke 11: 9). Afterwards the young man began to pray. I felt the working of the Holy Spirit upon me but I did not know how to open up to allow Him to speak out of me.

When I got off the phone I went back to my room and said to the Lord, "If this gift of the Baptism of the Holy Ghost is of You, give it to me." The Lord spoke audibly to me and then confirmed to me through the scriptures, "If you can believe on me as the scripture has said, out of your belly shall flow rivers of living water" (John 7:38).

I began to praise the Lord. In my mind I was saying, "Thank You Lord, I love You Father, I bless Your Holy Name". But when I listened to myself and heard the words coming from my mouth, it was not English, but another language. I was filled with the Holy Ghost with the evidence of speaking in another language. My life had truly changed. I possessed power to live right.

A New Church and Called into the Ministry

I went back to the Pentecostal church and testified that I was saved and filled with the Holy Ghost. I declared His Word says it was mine for the asking. I did not stay at this church long. God used this ministry as a schoolmaster, the law, to bring me to Christ.

Later, much chaos occurred in that church that resulted in it being divided so I began attending a church that was closer to my house. The people were very sincere and loving. This church focused on deliverance. Many people would come from near and far to be delivered from satanic possession.

I was called into the ministry under the covering of this particular ministry. In a vision, this pastor (now Bishop Demetrics Roscoe) had presented me with a gift, a present. The present was beautifully wrapped. When I opened it the word 'Prophetess' was spelled out. I looked at the word and the Spirit of God began to shake me literally and God spoke in a loud voice that probably only I could hear, "Prophesy My Word to My people."

The first person God told me to inform that He had called me into the ministry was my Dad (God does have a sense of humor). My Dad definitely would not have been on the top of my list to tell. I was aware that my Dad was taught through his denomination that God did not call women to preach. What a misinterpretation of the scripture, understanding that God calls willing vessels – not male or female.

My dad had previously stated that he thought I was losing my mind with all these religious practices such as praying for hours in my room throughout the week, fasting and no longer desiring things that appealed to the flesh. But when I told my dad that God had called me to preach, his words to me were and I quote, "If God said preach His Word, you should preach". I could only say, "Yes God, You are real."

Searching For More Leads To Meeting My Husband

Although, the Spirit of the Lord moved intensely at this church I began to be in search for more of a breakdown of the Word of God. I desired a greater revelation of Jesus Christ.

There was a new ministry that had moved from Bessemer to my side of town. It was a 'Word' emphasis church – a teaching ministry. I joined this church. I grew tremendously from the teaching of the Word. Later I became a part of the counseling department. After coming into the knowledge of Christ, I began to enjoy evangelism, witnessing to the lost, leading the lost through the sinner's prayer and getting them delivered. We would educate the people on their identity, purpose and destiny.

The young man that was over one aspect of the counseling department was very dedicated and persistent. He was a true devil chaser. I was very impressed with his zeal for the things of God. He was also good-looking, well dressed, truly saved and sold-out for Jesus – and can you believe, an eligible bachelor. God soon rewarded him for his faithfulness. After several months of working together in the ministry, God took the relationship between this young man and me in a new direction. We became attracted to one another. God sent him a ministry companion; one with his same passion for ministry. A year later we were married.

I met my husband, Wayne, at More Than Conquerors Faith Church (MTC), in Birmingham, Alabama. He is a native of the city of Birmingham. As strange as it may seem, we were raised in nearby neighborhoods and went to the same high school but never met during that time. Our first meeting was at the church – God's timing. Wayne is an only child and I am the seventh of nine. Nine plus one, divided by two, equals five, God's grace. Just like God, huh?

We both worked in the Counseling Department. Wayne was the director. Although I was active in the ministry prior to joining MTC, the church rules were that every new member had to go through Disciple's Training before being released to minister under their auspices. I was always inspired and motivated for ministry through Wayne's teaching and demonstration of deliverance.

He was very knowledgeable of God's Word and knew how to make his subject matters interesting to his students. Signs followed his teachings (word) when he would pray for those who needed deliverance. Many demons were cast out in the counseling room of the church.

Candidates came to the counseling room for salvation, receiving the baptism of the Holy Spirit, restoration or prayer. Wayne taught that a person needed to be delivered from demonic activity. If their spirit was not clean beforehand, he or she could not receive the Baptism of the Holy Spirit. As a result, on many occasions, services upstairs in the church would have ended but we would still be downstairs "casting out devils".

The other counselors often referred to Wayne as the "demon killer" because he was adamant about casting the devil out of those who were in bondage. We would stay late praying for people after church and many times we would carry that same anointing to restaurants and see God set the captive free there as well.

God saw Wayne's faithfulness and soon promoted him to Assistant Pastor at another Ministry. From there he went to being asked by a long time friend and Pastor,

Ed Kirkland, to serve as an interim Pastor of one of Pastor Kirkland's affiliated churches. We became the Senior Pastors and served there five years. Nearing the end of the fifth year, Wayne felt that the Lord had called him into the inner-city ministry. He resigned and started His Word Ministries Church.

Our first location was in the project area in the recreation center. After two years God blessed us with a building in downtown, Birmingham, where we are presently housed. We work very well together in ministry.

CHAPTER 5

My husband, Wayne

Wayne was never a very talkative – small talk – kind of individual. He mainly spoke when he was asked a question, and then gave you a direct answer. To get him to engage in a conversation, your subject had to be about the Bible or cars. He has always been this kind of person. He rarely would be the one to start a conversation – unless he felt that you might be interested in salvation or cars.

Our marriage journey has been one that many can learn from. The Lord began training us concerning marriage, through His Word.

Even before my husband and I met, God instructed me to allow Him to choose my mate. How? Through His

Word. What do I mean by that? Many people are confused about choosing a mate, thinking God points them out with His finger. He set His line-up. What He actually does is outline their characteristics in His Word. He gives us the description of a godly wife in Proverbs 31.

The Bible also describes the characteristics of them who are born again in Galatians 5:17. Once you see these signs in a believer, you can choose. Mind you, the pick is amongst <u>believers</u>. A believer should never, under any circumstances, choose their mate amid unbelievers (2Corinthians 6:14). It doesn't matter who his or her parents might be, what they have to offer, what they look like or even what church they may be affiliated with. The Word of God must always be the qualifying factor. The Word must be in them in abundance.

When I met Wayne, I did not immediately think of what God had told me about letting Him choose my mate. I knew he was marriage material, just not for me. I knew what I was looking for. I had already predetermined how much money my husband would make, his skin color, his height and even his education level. Therefore, in my mind, Wayne was not a candidate. I thank God today that I was not led by my mind, but by God's Spirit.

Wayne is everything any woman could hope for in a Christian mate. When we recited our wedding vows, we both agreed that we would stand with each other in sickness and in health. During my recovery from the heart attack in 2009, I found out how real these words were to Wayne. He was my caregiver. He took care of me both day and night. He was assisted by two of my sisters in helping out when he could not be there.

One of the key factors that I held to was that it was of the utmost importance that I marry a man who loved me. His love for me had to exceed even what I thought I would be able to give him in return. God tells husbands in Ephesians 5:25 that they are to love their wives as He loved the church and gave Himself for it. He tells wives that they are to reverence their husbands. I knew that I was going to honor God in my marriage and therefore obey His Word concerning my husband. He would be reverenced. I also knew that I could not control anyone other than myself and therefore it was important that my husband's love for me was based on God's Word.

The Bible talks about four kinds of Love:

1. Eros: Romantic love - love between husband and wife
2. Agape: Unconditional love – God kind of Love
3. Philo: Brotherly Love
4. Storge': Family, Friendship

He had to love me with the Agape and Eros kind of love. God gave me just that. I admit I was spoiled in my dating relationship. I felt that I had to be in control at all times which was not productive for a healthy relationship. The Bible states in first Corinthians that you must submit one to another. One thing for sure we both went into the marriage agreeing that God's Word would have the first and the final authority in our lives.

We both enjoy ministry. Everything we have ever received came by faith. The scripture states that the just shall live by faith (Habakkuk 2:4). God wants us to live by faith in every area of our lives.

Many are ignorant to the fact that the system is designed to help us fail. We feel that the American dream is living in a six figure home, two new cars, a flat screen television in every room and new kitchen appliances, as well as all of the latest technologies (i.e. cell phones and video games for our children). We feel this denotes that "we have arrived" without counting the cost.

People make mistakes attempting to be spiritual – especially in the area of finances. We believe God to save souls, deliver and set people free – but not to provide material things when it was in our power to acquire them. Unfortunately, that is where many couples go wrong.

We must understand that *'things'* must be paid for. Getting them is not impressive – the ability to keep them and yet spend time with your family . The god of this world is satan. He has a plot and plan in place that involves our economy. He strategizes that once we acquire all of these things that we honestly can't afford, we will have to get two jobs to keep them. This will take us away from our families and cause our children to be left alone.

The Bible states in Proverbs 29:15 that a son left to himself bring his parents to shame. How? Well, without the watchful eye of mom or dad, they will more than likely get with the wrong crowd. This could lead to stealing, drug use, premarital sex and other wrong choices. While parents are busy trying to pay for **things**, our children need us...our advice, guidance and most of all, our presence. They need us – not more *things*.

The reality is we get impatient and don't wait on God to bless us with these things. We sign on the dotted line and walk out with them forgetting that every thirty days payments are due. This was one of the major financial traps people fall for, but praise God for second and third chances.

Another tactic of the enemy is to use the things/people of God that you love and your service to God to deceive you. The adversary will lead us to think that it is God's will to abandon your first ministry (your family) to better serve others.

The family unit is the first ministry that God has assigned all of His children to. I don't care what role you serve in church, your first ministry is always your family. I believe that anyone who is involved in ministry can be susceptible to this.

It is easy for ministers to get caught-up in what goes on outside of the home: the church programs, prison ministry, and evangelistic outreach. While these things are important, our priorities must be in order. Family is important to God. He sent Jesus so that we would have the choice to be a part of His family if we so desired. We should always make sure that we are not abandoning our spousal and parental responsibilities. Remember that God tells us that 'one that does not provide for his family is worse than an infidel' (1Timothy 5:8). This is not restricted to financial provisions, but also spiritual teachings and instructions to your family.

When I met Wayne, he was employed as a welder and repaired cars on the side. He also raced cars. He later became a manager for Auto Zone. God was preparing him for destiny. He resigned from Auto Zone after having been requested to work on Sundays. He made a choice to step out on faith; a good idea but not a God-inspired idea. No preparation or much thought went into it. A word to the wise, "count the cost". This was truly a challenging time for us. We experienced serious financial setbacks. The scripture states, "make your plans within, and then build your house" (Proverbs 24:27).

Consequently, Wayne started an automotive detail service to help with the finances, but we soon found out this was not what God was saying. God had a different plan. God wants us to acknowledge Him and He will direct our steps (Proverbs 3:6).

We were out driving one day and we stopped at this particular automotive repair shop to inquire about a problem we were having with our car. While in the shop, Wayne and the owner got into a conversation. The owner told Wayne that he could successfully manage an automotive repair shop with his knowledge. He offered him a job. Two years after managing the shop this same owner wanted out and he offered us the business. We prayed about it and acquired the business.

In our sixteenth year of marriage, God supernaturally gave us our own automotive repair shop with no money down and bad credit. Yes, gave. With men these things are impossible, but with God all things are possible (Matthew19:26).

God spoke to a brother to fund our business. He put the upfront money necessary. He didn't want any part in the business. He just wanted to be a blessing and help wherever he could. His words were that God spoke to him to furnish the man of God's vision. God is good! God always has a person who will hear His voice and obey.

After my retirement from the Board of Education, I went to work part-time with Wayne at our automotive business. I worked at least three days each week. I would assist him with the daily operations. The other two days I would do the work of the ministry either making calls, hospital and nursing home visits, or counseling with those who needed guidance on one day and on the other day I would substitute teach.

I have always led a very active life. My husband and I are usually together all day, six out of seven days a week. My family would often comment, concerning our being together, "If we see one of you, we know the other one is somewhere near or on the way." We pray together and we play together. And this is what we have found is the ingredients for a healthy marriage. This is what we both prayed for.

Two years after my husband and I were wed, we prayed about conceiving a child. After several unsuccessful attempts, while yet enjoying the rehearsal, we decided to go to the doctor. I was told that I had fibroids on my ovaries that were preventing conception.

The doctor reluctantly gave me the infertility drug; but stated that he felt it would not work. I needed to have surgery. Surgery would only give me a fifty percent chance of conception. I wanted one hundred percent, and I realized that man could not provide that. Yet, I knew a man that could, and His name is Jesus.

In addition to the infertility drug, my husband and I got busy. He went through the Bible listing all the promises of God concerning children. We daily made our confessions, "And Jesus answered saying to them "Have faith in God". Truly I say to you, whoever says to this mountain 'Be taken up and cast into the sea and does not doubt in his heart, but believes that what he says is going to come to pass, he shall have whatsoever he saith. Therefore I say unto you, whatsoever you pray and ask, Believe that you receive it, and you shall have it" (Mark 11: 22-24).

"Again I say unto you that if two of you shall agree on earth touching anything that they shall ask, it shall be done for them by the father, who is in heaven" (Matthew 18:19).

The rest of our confessions were:

Now unto him that is able to do exceeding abundantly above all that we ask or think, according to the power that worketh in us,(Ephesians 3:20)

He maketh the barren woman to keep house, and to be a joyful mother of children. Praise ye the LORD. (Psalms 113:9)

Lo, children are an heritage of the LORD: and the fruit of the womb is his reward. (Psalms 127:3)

Thy wife shall be as a fruitful vine by the sides of thine house: thy children like olive plants round about thy table. Behold, that thus shall the man be blessed that feareth the LORD. (Psalms 128:3-4)

And whatsoever we ask, we receive of him, because we keep his commandments, and do those things that are pleasing in his sight. (1John 3:22)

After eight months of consistent confessions and walking it out (believing that we had received), God proved Himself to be faithful. Four children later, without any surgery by taking God at His Word He gave us our heart's desire. We allowed patience to have her perfect work (James 1:4). We became complete and in want of no promises of God. We proved Him and found Him to be a rewarder of those who diligently sought Him. (Hebrew 11:6)

He miraculously ended the process. I had a miscarriage after my fourth child. It was a disappointing time but I soon got over it. If God had seen fit to give us another child we would have gladly accepted His will; even though, we were no longer praying for another child. We felt that we had heard the Spirit say, "Well done" (or we told the Spirit, it's done).

The strangest thing was that neither Wayne nor I was willing to have the operation to finalize child conception. We had discussed it, but neither one of us wanted to do it. So we prayed about it and God closed my womb without any surgery, no birth control, and still we had marital relations when we wanted to. God can do just what you can believe Him to do.

CHAPTER 6
Ministry Works

In 2003, God blessed me to birth my own women's ministry, Honoring Every Resurrected Sister (H.E.R.S). Through this ministry, we would minister to the women in the Birmingham Work Release Program. These were women who had recently been released from prison. This facility served as a halfway house. It was used to help make the transition of the women back to society through family connection and or employment.

We would minister at the half way house on the third Sunday evening of each month delivering the message of hope. We stressed that delay does not mean denial. On holidays we would carry gifts, consisting of needed items, to the women to show them the love of their Father. We would have a special time of fellowshipping with them around God's Word.

Through H.E.R.S, we would minister at the Love Lady's Center in Birmingham, sharing the Word of God to the families housed there. These were a very diverse group of people that found themselves there due to various circumstances. Some were mothers with children with no income that had recently been released from prison. Many were substance abuse victims undergoing rehabilitation. Some were just simply unemployed.

God spoke to me, "Just as you have been forgiven and restored, teach others of My forgiveness and restoration power. Be an example of My love in the earth." And through this ministry, after we deliver the Word, the Lord works with us, confirming His Word with signs and miracles following (Mark 16:20).

One thing that has really blessed me is Wayne's acceptance of my ministry. Wayne has never seemed to be threatened by it. He has given me the liberty to obey God. He is comfortable with my going forth. People have often mistaken his confidence with weakness. He has often stated that we are to complete one another, never to compete with one another. He knows who he is, whose he is and what he has been called to do. He is not intimidated by anyone else's gifting. Our ministries are fulfilled in Christ.

CHAPTER 7

My Heart Attack on Christmas 2009

December 25, 2009 started out as an ordinary Christmas morning. I got up and prepared breakfast for the family. After clearing away the dishes, I informed the children that we would have our annual Christmas program in the family room around 10:00 am.

During the program all the children had their individual terms of stating "What Christmas Means to Them". Afterwards, we sang Christmas Carols then dismissed in prayer. Now this is where my life takes a turn.

Around 1:00 pm, the children had gone to their rooms. I was still sitting downstairs. I felt a little thirsty so I went and got a Diet Pepsi, something I seldom drink. After one swallow I felt a discomfort in my chest area. I can only describe it as tightness. I tried to move about a little to see if it would pass but immediately the tightness spread to my left arm which began to feel numb.

I went to lie down to see if that would help the pain to subside. That's when a commercial from the American Heart Association that I had seen came to my mind. They were interviewing people from various walks of life, male and female, young and old. They all said "I feel fine, I feel fine", not knowing they were about to have a heart attack. The commercial further spoke about numbness in your left arm and tightness in your chest. It had stated that you should see your physician if these things occurred. I attempted to fight the thought that was in my mind concerning going to the doctor. After all, it was Christmas Day. But the pain persisted...

While I was lying on the sofa, my husband (not realizing that anything was going on with me), said that he would be back in a couple of hours. Jeremiah's other granddaddy's car had stopped, and he and his family were stranded. My husband had told him that he was on his way, not realizing that he would not make it. I told my husband that I thought I should go to the emergency room to be checked out. I told him that I did not feel right and I described my symptoms.

My husband immediately knew it must be serious because I was never sick. I was not on any medication and had always led a very busy lifestyle: Co-Pastor of our church, Co-owner of our family automotive service, very involved with the educational system, volunteer at my children's school and hands-on with our four very active teenagers. He readily agreed that we should go and get it checked out. We realized that it was Christmas Day and that my doctor's office would be closed, so we went to the emergency room. I felt that we could go ahead and get back in time to attend our family Christmas dinner at my sister's house.

After arriving at the emergency room we went to the counter and signed in. The clerk asked what was going on. When I told her my symptoms she immediately called me to the back and took my vital signs. They did an electrocardiogram (EKG).

One thing that I find strange is one of the doctors came and talked with us and told us that there was some good news, "It was not my heart." But much to my surprise, and theirs how mistaken they were. Thanks unto God for abnormal blood work because this caused them to keep me overnight for observation.

Many tests were run and the echocardiogram revealed that I had indeed experienced a heart attack. The doctors proceeded with surgery by attempting to place stents in my heart to eliminate the blockage. They regretfully informed my husband and me that the procedure was unsuccessful. Now this is where my story gets even more interesting...

A Lose-Lose Situation

A specialist was called in. He examined my heart x-rays. Afterwards, he sympathetically stood over my bed, looked me in the face and declared, "Mrs. Taylor it doesn't look good. I must be honest with you. It doesn't look promising either way. The facts are, if we wait and do nothing, the damage that has already been done to your heart could be fatal and you could die. On the other hand, if we attempt to operate, it could be fatal because your heart is already agitated. If we attempt to correct or repair your heart it could easily just shut down."

Now, just stop and sigh with me. Can you imagine being told by a professional that you are in a 'lose-lose' situation? You have to know, that you know, that you know, the Lord! I asked to see my husband. Thank God for a husband who knows how to believe in Him.

We began to pray and put God in remembrance of His Word. My husband called my family members to inform them of what had happened. They were all in disbelief, recalling that they had just spoken with me about seeing them at the dinner. I, too, thought about how I was looking forward to attending my grandbaby's two-year-old birthday party that Saturday. I had spoken to his mother that day and told her not to postpone it. I just knew that I would be out of the hospital in time to attend. Again remember, I thought that I would be given some medicine and released. With all of these plans in place, the hospital trip was not on the schedule.

Needless to say, my family dropped everything else and all roads led to the hospital. They immediately came. Wayne proceeded to call his prayer intercessors. They came as far as Sumter County, Tuscaloosa and all over the cities of Alabaster and Birmingham.

One thing that we are convinced of is that the effectual prayer of the righteous, those who live what they confess, would avail much (James 5:16). He called those who were strong and knew their God so they could do great exploits" (Daniel 11:32). He called those who he knew would pray and not faint, or be moved by what they saw or heard.

Our Assistant Pastor, at that time, had the church to pray daily for me. She wrote out a confession for them. Not only were they to confess it out loud daily, but also every Wednesday and Sunday when they came together corporately. She declared that they would confess God's

Word concerning me until I came back to church and resumed my praise.

So as the cardiologist (heart Doctor) stood over me with his report, asking the question, and waiting on a response, "What do you want me to do?" I just smiled and said, "You do what you can do and my God will do the rest". He then asked, "Does that mean go ahead and do the surgery?" and I said "yes". My husband and I had to sign a release form that we would not hold the hospital liable, if I did not make through the surgery. I get excited today as I think about how God took me off the scene and He replied for me.

Calling the 'Specialist'

God used the cardiologist, Dr. M. K. Goyal, who was on duty to his extent. Dr. Goyal initially proceeded to correct the visible problem. He put the balloon and stents in my heart and thought that he had corrected the problem. But the procedure failed. Saints, *'Life Is Not Over, Until God Says It's Over'*.

They had to rush me back into surgery. Dr. Goyal looked at the x-rays, called my husband in and told him that it didn't look good and that he needed to call in the specialist. My husband later told me that Dr. Goyal might not have known but he had already called up the specialist.

My husband had the saints on post praying around the clock. Our ministry's intercessor, Prophetess Candis, had phoned my husband after getting the word about my condition informing him that the Lord said that we will recover all. That word along with a word from his close friend, Prophet Leon Lee, confirmed that he was to stay positioned on the wall until I came out. Dr. Goyal's specialist was named Riggins but my husband's specialist is named Jesus.

My friend, Sister Cynthia, an intercessor, along with her son Christopher stayed at my home for over a week praying and believing God for my speedy recovery. Christopher who was seventeen then, told my sons, "This is serious. We can't be playing now. We must be in prayer for your mother." Cynthia told me that he was in sincere prayer for me. God honored that child-like faith.

There's a songwriter who puts it like this, "In times like these, you have to be sure and very sure that your anchor holds and that you grip a solid rock." You can't have uncertain or wavering faith. You have to have had some experience with the faithfulness of God to sustain you. Hebrews describes faith as the substance of things hoped for and the evidence of things not seen (Hebrews 11:1).

My substance at that moment was the Word of God that had been hid in my heart, and my previous testimonies of the delivering power of God. My evidence would be the fruitlessness of man's report.

As I listened to the doctor's report, I could imagine how David felt when he had to go up against Goliath. His strength and faith came from past experiences with God's victory. When faced with this new challenge, Goliath, he reflected on when he was in the field attending his father's sheep and a lion and a bear came to attack the sheep. David relied on God and with his bare hands, God allowed him to retrieve the sheep out of the bear and lion's mouth. He knew that if God, through him could do that, Goliath would be brought down by the power of God as well (1Samuel 17:34-35).

I remembered nothing else that happened on the earth or in the operating room. God made me to lie down. While the surgery was being performed He gave me an out-of-body experience.

CHAPTER 8

The Out of Body Experience!

This chapter is the heart of this book. It is why this book has been written. Prayerfully read this chapter and take heed to what took place during my surgery. Please don't take this experience lightly. Get ready!

While on the operating table my spirit came out of my body. I saw my body on the table but at the same time I was in a courtroom. There were four people in the courtroom beside myself, a judge, one witness and two attorneys. I was on trial. It was like the Judgment day.

The prosecuting attorney stated his case against me. He represented the law. He stated all the things that I had done in the flesh. I sat in amazement. Many times I thought, "How did he know that?" After he rested his case the judge nodded to the other attorney who was apparently defending me. My attorney's opening argument was, "Yes, these things are true but the price has already been paid. She accepted Jesus as her Savior and Lord. He paid the price for her redemption" (Ephesians 1:7).

I sat there in disbelief realizing that they were discussing me. His closing statement was, "All of her sins and transgressions are now 'Under the Blood" (1John 1:7).

When both sides had rested their cases, the judge looked at me and stated that the verdict was in my favor and then he asked me, "Which way will you have this to go?" He informed me that I had a choice to leave now and enter into heaven or stay. There was such a peace that came over me. I thought, I could be out of here; no more sickness, no more sorrow, no more pain, no more disappointments, and no more dealing with people that seemingly do not want to be helped.

On the other hand, I thought grief of knowing that one day your loved one will die. Just when I was leaning to seemingly say, "I am out of here". I said, "I will stay". The judge inquired, "How long"? I pondered in my mind, "Should I say two months, two years, or ten years?" All of a sudden out of my mouth, I said, "I'll wait on the Rapture".

The judge looked at me and said, "The Rapture"? Then he opened a big book that was sitting on his desk; he looked into it and looked back at me and again said, "The Rapture, that time won't be long either. Go back and preach the Kingdom of God is at Hand". The witness said only one thing, "She will tell the Good News". The last thing I remembered was the judge stating, "So be it" – and my spirit went back into my body.

I remembered being awakened by a nurse to ask me how I felt. I explained to her that there was a burning in my chest. She responded that this could not be because they had completed the surgery. I declared again that there was still a burning in my chest.

My husband later told me that they had to perform surgery a second time and do a quadruple bypass. There were four blocked arteries. The surgeons worked on two of the four arteries in the first surgery and sent me to recovery. Then they discovered, only by the Holy Spirit, that the stents and balloon had both failed.

Satan had plotted a backup plan for my demise. In view of the fact that he couldn't destroy me with the heart attack; he knew if they did not do the entire bypass that they still could lose me. But my God had an upfront plan. God had already declared in His Word that I should live and not die and declare the wondrous work of the Lord

(Psalms 118:17). Furthermore, no weapon (heart attack, cancer, stroke, diabetes, nor any other disease) formed against me – His elect – shall prosper (take me out). God has given His angels charge over us to keep us in all our ways (Psalms 91:11; Isaiah 54:17). Satan thought he had an infallible plan.

I had fibroids removal surgery (Laparoscopic Hysterectomy) three weeks prior to the heart attack. It was a one-day surgery. In preparation for this surgery I had an electrocardiogram (EKG) performed, blood work drawn, a stress test and cholesterol test. I was given a clean bill of health. I was back to my usual routine in less than a week. I underwent the surgery with no complications and I was part of a twenty-five year cardiac (heart) program through a major research at the University of Alabama at Birmingham (UAB); only three weeks later to experience all of this.

See, I know and accept that I am a threat to satan. He feels that if he can get me out of the picture, earth, that he would have a greater chance of destroying more people. However, if I remain; I will do the work of the ministry, lead the lost to Christ, pray for the sick and see them recover and cast out devils (Mark 16:17). Satan didn't stop there either, I found out mysteriously, during the second operation, fluid filled my lungs and the surgeons had to go through my back to drain off the fluid.

The Heart Surgeon

I had a strong desire to meet with the heart surgeon. There were questions that would often go through my mind concerning the procedure. I needed to talk to the man that God had equipped to perform the operation that could have brought about life or death for me. Four months after my surgery, my sister and I went back to the hospital and visited the floor where my surgery took place.

My sister Marilyn remembered just about all of the staff and each room where I had stayed. She and my baby sister Renaye took shifts when my husband could not be there taking care of me. The experience was somewhat frightening and emotional for me. There was so much I did not remember. We spoke to some of the staff that helped nurse me back to health. Yes, many remembered me; as one nurse stated when I asked, "Do you remember me?" Her response was, "How could we not remember you? You are the miracle patient."

I was so deeply touched when I saw the other patients on this floor. Some I embraced and told them that they would be just fine. I wanted to just camp there for the whole day just to encourage them. But I know for sure that I will be going back, especially on this coming Christmas Day and Christmas' hereafter, to let the patients know '**That Life's Not Over Until God's Says It's Over**' and to leave them a copy of this book.

Each day when I leave my house we have to pass by Shelby Baptist Hospital. My husband, my children and I never fail to make mention in prayer, by extending our hands toward the hospital to request healing for the cardio patients that must undergo heart surgery. Now all of that was good and needful, but it still did not suffice the need I had to talk with the cardiovascular physician.

I scheduled an appointment to see Dr. Riggins. I had to wait over an hour to see, not him, but one of his associates. I was told that Dr. Riggins had been called to the hospital for an emergency. He is very much in demand.

The team member had my records with him and he felt that he could explain the procedure and answer any questions that I may have had. I was so disappointed. He was quite cordial; but he was not who I came to talk to. He was very knowledgeable about the general procedure, but that was not what I needed. I came for specifics.

We were kind to each other, but even without my saying so, he knew I needed to talk with Dr. L. Shefton Riggins. I thanked him for his time and left. I left out of his presence thinking and laughing with my husband saying, "I double-dog-dare him to send me a bill because I didn't ask to see him" (smile, just kidding).

I never set up another appointment. I prayed about it going home and put it in God's hands. I told my husband, "God knows I want to meet with Dr. Riggins, and somehow God is going to make it happen". The next day

Dr. Riggins' receptionist phoned me to set up an appointment because he wanted, personally, to talk with me about the procedure (look at God).

During my interview in Dr. Riggins office, I asked him four pertinent questions which he promptly answered. I asked, "What was noted as my prognosis"? He stated that I had a condition called a Coronary Artery Dissection# (my arteries had separated) and there was very limited blood flow.

Taylor: "After being called in and viewing the x-rays, what came to your mind"?

Riggins: "This was an emergency situation and I had to begin the operation immediately".

Taylor: Do you believe in miracles?

Riggins: "Yes".

Taylor: "What will you allow me to quote you saying concerning my outcome?"

Riggins: "My gift; I say gift because I know the ability to repair a person's heart comes from God. I asked God when I was five years of age to make me a doctor and He did just that. There can be two individuals of the same age, same physical health and all other factors being equal, I can perform the same procedure on both individuals; one lives and the other dies. Through this unexplainable, in the natural occurrence, I have come to know that Jesus determines a man's or woman's life cycle, not me. I love my work and through it I have come to see the power and ability of God."

I shared with Dr. Riggins my out of body experience while undergoing surgery. His statement to me was; "I believe that you were left here for a reason and you must obey God. Warn the people to prepare for the Rapture (the coming of the Messiah) – whether it is when their name alone is called, or the great call away."

God can speak louder than any human. Make your request to God and wait for the answer. Interviewing with the number one heart surgeon in the country, Dr. Riggins – as my sister asked, "How did that happen? Can anything great come out of a hospital in Alabaster?"

My family felt that I should have been taken to University of Alabama at Birmingham Hospital, or one of the larger hospitals in Birmingham. But since we live in Alabaster we went to the closest hospital. I found out a long time ago, it is when God gets into a thing, whether the thing is great or small He makes the difference. God got into a small hospital and brought about great things.

CHAPTER 9

Obedience

One Wednesday during Bible Study I was instructed by the Holy Spirit to teach on Obedience. My first quest was to poll the saints, which included my four teenage children of their definition of 'obedience'. As a mother and a Pastor, I strive very diligently to get my children to participate in church affairs with the right attitude.

I realize that people expect more from Preacher's Kids. I accept the fact that I have my work cut out for me. I have observed my teens many times in church when they were not playing their instruments. They seemed either preoccupied in their minds or totally bored. I have taken the task on many occasions to see where their minds are.

One attempt had been that I asked the straightforward question, "Do you love Jesus?" As always they answered, "Yes." But when asked, "Why do you refuse to show the signs, because 'love' is an action word?" My second oldest who is never lost for words replied, "We don't want to be at church all the time." (I think all parents have at least one of these blessings also.)

The Bible tells us, as parents, to train up (show and instruct) a child in the way he should go, and when he is old he will not depart (stray) from it (the truth or the path) (Proverbs 22:6). I attempted to passionately explain to them that we are commissioned by God to carry them to church (the ecclesia) to hear God's Word, but that we cannot to make them believe it. Our job is only to position them to hear truth. It is the job of the Holy Spirit's job to do the convincing.

The scripture tells us in 1Corinthians 3:6 that one soweth the Word, another waters it but God gives the increase. Through that we know, as an old cliché also states, "You can lead a horse to water but you can't make him drink." We put our children in the environment, and it takes God to open up their hearts to receive. We can take them to church but we can't make them worship. You can carry a horse to the water but you can't make him drink.

Now, after presenting the question to my second oldest son, "What is obedience to you?" His response was,

"Doing what is expected of you". That was not exactly the answer I was looking for, but I immediately considered the source. After a short pause, after hearing my son's response, I was directed to ask Disciple Desiree# who defined obedience as doing what you are told, when you are told, how you are told, because you are told. My response was, "Let the Church say, Amen!"

Disciple Desiree is a young lady who is very dedicated, loyal and dependable. She, her mom and brothers have been with us since the conception of the ministry. Many have come and gone but she and her family are a part of those who have remained faithful. Therefore, I knew she would have a 'God-inspired' definition of the term 'obedience'.

This teaching took place around the third week of December. Shortly after this we began to prepare for our church's annual Christmas program and our family's annual Christmas Eve program which was held at my mom's house.

Every Christmas Eve for the past forty years, my mother and father have gathered me and my eight siblings together to celebrate the Christmas holiday. My father always had to work on Christmas Day; so, we had to get up early Christmas morning, and gather around their bed, and say our prayers and thank the Lord for what we had received, even if very little. We were thankful for having received something.

We were considered poor, but we didn't know we were poor. So we were very grateful for having received a pair of roller skates, a new doll or a second-hand bike. We would be so excited to have something different to play with. We could not unwrap any of the toys until we had prayed. After the prayer, pleading in our mind that it would be short, we would launch into our toys.

Meanwhile, my father smiled as he hurriedly rushed off to work. So my mother came up with the suggestion to have our Christmas Family gathering on Christmas Eve so that my father could take part in the entire Family Christmas Celebration. Hence we started having our Christmas Program on Christmas Eve. We would exchange gifts and eat good food on Christmas Eve. This practice has been a continuous tradition of the Jones family. Today, even after my father's death in 1990, the tradition continues.

When we started this tradition I was approximately thirteen years old. Like most other young children my emphases was on the gifts, not the Giver of the true gift to the world. I did not know the true meaning of Christmas, so I expectantly anticipated opening presents and hearing the Christmas story, at that time, 'Santa & the Reindeers'.

Each year my oldest brother, 'Bro' (as we call him), would be in rare form. He would immaculately dress the part of Santa Claus, bringing the 'ho, ho, ho' sound of Santa; passing out candy canes to all the children with the lights lowered, and singing "Here comes Santa Claus" and "Jingle Bells". Now, this is where the obedience comes in.

Again let me remind you, a forty-year practice, custom, acceptance of family members, high anticipation of Santa story, setting the stage of events. Here comes the requirement of total obedience by God stating that He needs me to obey Him beyond popular opinion.

Earlier, we established that the definition of 'obedience' is doing what you are told; when you are told, how you are told, because you are told. Obedience has nothing to do with whether or not one agrees with what is required but more so with understanding authority, and knowing that all authority is given and ordained by God. Disobedience or obedience is not to a person but a position. The assignment is from a position of office.

For over thirty years I found enjoyment in the exchanging of gifts. After coming into truth and the realization that it was not that person's birthday, nor was there a need by the individual receiving my gift, I decided to walk in the true meaning of Christmas. Our giving was conditional. If the dollar value was not of equal or higher value than what had been spent by us, there could be great disappointment. I felt free!

The Bible states, "If you abide in me and my word abides in you (John 15:7), you are my disciples indeed (John 8:31), and you shall know the truth and the truth shall make you free (John 8:32) and whom the son set free, you are free indeed (John 8:36)." I no longer felt obligated to spend money I did not have. Charging presents to give to people and over-extending my budget. I would buy gifts one year and two years down the line I would be still paying for those gifts. Many times those gifts would be discarded or obsolete but I was still paying. The interest alone could double the cost.

God began to mandate me to obedience and to share truth with others. Although, initially I did not perceive it that way, I vividly recalled one of my family members saying I was a perpetrator. That pierced deeply. I pondered it in my heart. I remember while riding in the car on my way home, asking God, "Why did she refer to me as a perpetrator?" God spoke vividly, "My sheep hear My voice and obey, and those that are not of Me, hear their father's voice and obey". So in that light I was dispelling satan's voice and plans against my family. Therefore, I was definitely not on the welcoming committee of 'favorites', nor were they glad to see me coming. But through persistence, God allowed layers of tradition to be slowly unwrapped from my family's program year by year.

God first begin to reveal to us about celebrating the birth of the Savior into the world with the alcohol, cigarettes, and loud, ungodly music? After prayer and time, all of those types of activities were done away with. We exchanged all of that with the grandchildren and great-grandchildren putting on the Christmas Program. They read scriptures, sing songs, do a liturgical dance, recite a poem, or play their instruments, all to the Glory of God. The adults, nowadays, sing Christmas Carols and appoint someone to tell "What Christmas Means to Them"(Isaiah 40:31).

Now, we are partially revealed. One more river to cross. Now this is the big clincher. "Now yet one thing lacketh thou", as Jesus told the rich young ruler in Matthew 19:21; you have cleaned up and done well, **sell completely out** (paraphrased). "Come all the way in. You are at the point where all men will know that you belong to Me".

There are many Christians who don't mind getting saved or changed but they don't want their friends, associates, to know that they are 'one of them' now, the good guys. They still want to feel that they can fit in, be accepted, and not be different.

"But ye are a chosen generation, a royal priesthood, an holy nation, **a peculiar people***, that ye should show forth the praises of him who hath called you out of darkness into his marvelous light.* *"Which in time past were not a people, but are now the people of God, which had not obtained mercy, but now have obtained mercy"* (1Peter 2:9-10). Exposing fooling the very elect, if possible (Matthew 24:24); *rather believing a lie than the truth* (2Thessalonians 2:11).

The Wednesday prior to our annual Christmas Eve program at my parents' house in 2009, my second oldest brother came by our automotive shop. He said that he needed a big favor from me. I could not imagine what the favor could be. He said that he wanted me to give the meaning for the season at our annual Christmas Eve program. My mouth practically dropped into my lap. I agreed to do it. He was totally used by God for this request.

Before this year, I had been purposely left off the program because I was termed radical. But it was probably just my imagination. I believe if Jesus said it in His Word, that is what He meant.

I received a commission from God to expose darkness. We were to no longer teach our children the lie about Santa Claus – not even in a playful nor innocent way. The scriptures tell us if we tell it, or find pleasure in others who spread this lie; we are just as guilty (Ephesians 5:1-17). "And have no fellowship with the unfruitful works of darkness, but rather reprove (correct) them" (Ephesians 5:11). I was commissioned to reprove the family traditional Santa Claus story. Consequently I was said to be taking away the fun from the children, to being a party pooper, or raining on their parade.

God had been dealing with me in regards that He was soon to return, and that we must get our house in order. So He gave me a platform for that evening, to warn my family "to make ready for His return". Just like God, He set it up and placed me on program to obey Him.

The Bible states, "It is better to obey (fear) God more than man. For man can only destroy the body but not the soul. God can destroy both body and soul..." (Matthew 10:28). There comes a time in every believer's life that he or she must choose between obeying God or man. To obey God will cost you everything. One must be willing to lose his life, his favorable disposition, his ranking, even to be lied on, to walk in total obedience. To walk with the world is to be in enmity with God (James 4:4).

I obeyed God that night and I felt such freedom and the approval of God.

The next day, satan struck immediately. I had the heart attack. I declared earlier that one of the provisions of obedience is protection even from a severe attack to the heart because God is greater.

In Isaiah 54:17, God never said that the weapons wouldn't form, but He promised that they wouldn't 'prosper', for this is the heritage (promises) for the servants (disciples) of God. He said, "A thousand may fall at your side, and ten thousand at your right hand; but it shall not come nigh you" (my dwelling) (Psalms 91:7). They wouldn't prevail. "For He has given His Angels charge over us to keep all of His employees safe" (Psalms 91:11).

Now the question is "Are you an employee, disciple, of Jesus?" I believe my being alive today is because of the favor I have found in the sight of God due to total obedience. God further states in Psalms 91:8-10 when you walk in obedience to His Word, "Only with your eyes shall you see the rewards, punishments of the wicked. Because you have made the Lord, who is my Refuge, Even the most High, your dwelling place. No evil shall befall you; nor shall any plague come nigh your dwelling."

The rest of the promises to the disciples, whom we are, for being obedient to His Word (voice), are recorded in verses 12 -16 of Psalms 91.

> *They shall bear thee up in their hands, lest thou dash thy foot against a stone. Thou shalt tread upon the lion and adder: the young lion and the dragon shalt thou trample under feet. Because he hath set his love upon me, therefore will I deliver him: I will set him on high, because he hath known my name. He shall call upon me, and I will answer him: I will be with him in trouble; I will deliver him, and honour him. With long life will I satisfy him, and shew him my salvation (Psalms 91:12-16).*

Also See:

1. Salvation: Acts 8: 26-28
2. Healing: 2Kings 5:1-10, 14
3. Righteousness: Genesis 12:1-5, 22:1-3
4. Protection/Safety: Genesis 6:7-8

5. Prosperity: Joshua 1:8
6. Long Life: Exodus 20:12; Proverbs 6:20-23; Ephesians 6:1-3
7. Deliverance: Proverbs 21:31; 2Timothy 4:18; Psalms 34:19

The scripture that came to mind is "when a man or woman ways (obedience) please the Lord He will make his enemies (last enemy to be conquered 'Death') to be in subjection." Death cannot take you out. As Jesus declared just before His time of departure, "no man nor circumstance take my life, but I choose to lay it down. I reserve the power to say 'when'". And I believe that in the life of a Disciple, those obedient to the cause, God allows us to also say "when". Ain't that good news?

CHAPTER 10

BEING ASSURED

The Revelation of Jesus Christ, which God gave him to show His servants things which must shortly come to pass. God sent and signified it by His Angel to His servant John, who bore witness to the Word of God, and to the testimony of Jesus Christ and to all things that he saw. Blessed is he who reads and those who hear the words of this prophecy, and keep those things which are written in it for the 'Time Is Near'. (Revelation 1:1-3 NKJV)

As I began to reflect back on Christmas Day 2009 and the heart attack, I had to have a heart to heart talk with

God. The whole essence surrounding the event could not be adequately explained. The parts were not fitly joined together. I soon concluded that this thing was bigger than what appeared. Figuratively speaking the heart attack could be described as a schoolmaster (law) that brought us into purpose.

As I looked back over my life there were so many obstacles set in my path that God overturned, intervened, or prevented that I'm convinced that He could have prevented the heart attack. But He decided to use what the devil meant for evil or my devastation to get an end-time message in the earth. So we must hear the conclusion of the matter and fear God and keep His commandments.

In writing this Book, in order to get the word out concerning the second coming of the Messiah, I was truly faced with numerous oppositions. I seem to have been fighting with unseen forces. Seemingly their objective was to hinder (kill, steal and destroy -attributes of satan) to cause others either not to receive nor heed the warnings.

The scripture tells us in Ephesians 6:12 that our fight is not against flesh and blood but against principalities, powers and rulers of the darkness in high places. Many times distraction may come from those closest to you. They fail to understand the underlying intents of the evil one, satan. He realizes that his sentencing has already been passed and he is now trying to deceive as many as possible to eternal damnation as well.

But God has come through His messenger to warn us to "make ready" and to assure each of us that God is real. He is alive and well, and hell is enlarging its borders. Jesus is on His way back and nothing but the pure in heart shall see our God.

In order to see Him as your righteous judge, you must come out of a world of sin realizing that you are a sinner. Not because of what you have done, but because of the condition for which you were born (sinful flesh). And therefore, you are in need of a Savior.

That is why in the third chapter of John, Jesus told Nicodemus "you must be born again". Jesus proceeded to tell him not through the natural birthing canal for that will only produce sinful flesh again but he must be born again of the Spirit and the water. To Be Born Again is not a natural process. It is the Lord's doing, once a man or woman makes their request for new life. In other words, heart transplant and a blood transfusion, our blood for His.

For all men are born sinners, but once they invite Christ into their heart, they become a new person in Christ Jesus. Old things are done away with and now all things are now new (2Corinthians 5:17) Romans 10: 9-10 states, if you confess with your mouth the Lord Jesus Christ and believe in your heart that God raised Jesus from the dead, thou shall be saved (delivered, protected, healed, provided for and have a new beginning). With the mouth (words spoken) confession is made unto salvation and with his heart, you believe unto right living. (Paraphrased)

Therefore we no longer have a need to worry about our lack of finances, physical prognoses, threat of divorce, loss of job, children outcome not favorable, failing because we now stand on the word of God and it tells us *"Its Not Over ..until God says Its Over..."*

Jesus said in Isaiah 40:10, "God is coming back with His reward with Him." He will judge the earth. With righteousness he shall judge the world; and with equity judge the people" (Psalm 98:9). Psalms 135:14 "For the Lord will judge His people and He will have compassion on His servants (those who are on His payroll, Those who He can count on to tell the Good News" (Psalms 135:14).

The scripture tells us in Revelation 1:7-8, "Behold he is coming with clouds, and every eye shall see Him, even they who pierced Him. And all the tribes of the earth will mourn because of Him. Even so, Amen. I am the Alpha and the Omega, the Beginning and the end, says the Lord, who is and who was, and who is to come, the Almighty."

Yes, Jesus will return to the earth and He will judge every man and the question is when your case is presented, as with me, what sins will confront you? Moreover, will you be justified by knowing the price having been paid and sealed by the Blood of Jesus?

The only way you can have this assurance, you must make Jesus both Savior and Lord – NOW! Not by just joining a church, being baptized in water but connecting to the Kingdom through acceptance of His works. If you want to have this assurance when you stand at the judgment and your case is presented, you must have made your calling and election sure. So before it is too late, you should pray this prayer with me, (read it out loud).

Dear Heavenly Father. I have read the testimony of Your servant, Patricia Taylor, and I believe that You have spared her life for such a time as this. I believe what You have revealed to her concerning Your Son, Jesus' soon return. I want to be ready to be received by Him. Therefore as stated in Your Word: I confess with my mouth that Jesus Is Lord and I believe in my heart that God raised Jesus from the dead. I repent of all of my sins and I ask You to cleanse me with Your blood. I invite You into my heart. Forgive me of my sins. Wash them all away – to remember no more.

Help me to now forgive myself as You have forgiven me. I do believe that Jesus died on the cross and on the third day His Father raised Him from the dead with all powers given unto Him, in both heaven and earth. Today, I accept You into my life to lead, instruct, and guide me to all truth.

Thank You, Father, for I am now to live a victorious life through you. I commit to reading Your Word daily, so I can grow thereby. I commit to daily prayer, communing with the Father and connecting with a local church, so I can assemble myself with other believers. Thank you, Father. My name is now written in the Lamb's Book of Life.

Then we who are alive and remain shall be "caught up" (Rapture) together with them in the clouds to meet the Lord in the air and thus we shall always be with the Lord (1Thessalonians 4:15-16). We therefore comfort You with these words. "Be Ready".

Jesus and all of heaven have been waiting on this moment. Write me or contact us for more information or to send us your testimony after accepting Jesus into your heart or to request more literature on living a life pleasing unto God. We want to hear from you.

Yours In Kingdom Service

Pastor Patricia J. Taylor

www.ingramcontent.com/pod-product-compliance
Lightning Source LLC
Chambersburg PA
CBHW051455290426
44109CB00016B/1765